Four Faces in Stone

A kid's book about carving Mount Rushmore

by Mildred Hopkins

M H Enterprises
Hominy, Oklahoma 74035

Library of Congress Catalog Card No. 83-90302

First Printing May 1983
Second Printing July 1984
Third Printing April 1986

Photos courtesy of National Park Service

Typography: Arrow Graphics
Layout: Stan Cohen

COVER PHOTO: The Mount Rushmore National Memorial carved by Gutzon Borglum, as it looks today. The four figures — George Washington, Thomas Jefferson, Theodore Roosevelt and Abraham Lincoln — were chosen to remind Americans of the greatness of their country and the men who helped build it.

PUBLISHED BY M H ENTERPRISES
420 West Fourth Street
Hominy, Oklahoma 74035

Chapter One

Many years before you were born — in 1924, to be exact — a group of men in the northwestern part of our country had a dream. They wished to carve a monument in the mountains of South Dakota, in the area called the Black Hills.

But who would be able to carve such a monument?

The men had heard of the work being done by a sculptor, Gutzon Borglum.

"This is the man we want," they said, and asked him if he could carve a monument there in the mountains out of rock that reached high up into the sky.

Borglum felt the job would be interesting, but he needed to see the mountains before he could give an answer. So, in the fall of 1924, he made a trip to the Black Hills to look over the area.

Riding horseback, with his 12-year-old son, Lincoln, beside him, and local men as guides, he wandered through the forests of Ponderosa pines, exploring the rocky areas of the Black Hills.

On that trip he found no spot suitable for a carving such as he planned.

A year later, however, Borglum went back to the Hills, and this time he was more successful. He set out once again on horseback with his son beside him. Their guide was Theodore Shoemaker, who had once been a sheriff, and knew every part of the Black Hills.

The group spent two weeks in the pine forests, camping by woodland streams each night and viewing the rock formations each day.

They climbed cliffs which seemed impossible to climb.

Finally, they came to one peak which was so high that it could be seen for miles. It caught the morning light and the sun shone on it much of the day.

It would be a mountain-climbing job to get to the top, however.

Three of the men were the first to scale the steep sides of the rock. There were so few places to hold on to that they had to use ropes to loop over trees and other rocks and pull themselves up. When they got near the top there were fewer trees to hook onto. At one point two of the men had to stand close to each other while the third man stood on their shoulders.

And remember, this was some 500 feet above the ground! One slip of the foot and one or all of them would go crashing to the ground below.

The man carefully threw a rope up over a rock and tied it securely. One by one the men pulled themselves up and over the top.

They were now on top of Mount Rushmore (once known as Slaughterhouse Rock). It was a huge mass of granite rock that rose some 500 feet higher than the hills and forests around it. It seemed to be reaching up into the sky.

This was where Borglum would carve his monument.

Opposite page: This is Mount Rushmore as artist Gutzon Borglum first saw it and decided to carve the faces here.

Chapter Two

Borglum told people about the spot he had chosen.

"But that's impossible," they said. "You can't carve a statue out of rock that high on a mountain. There is no way to get up to the top where you'd have to work. How would you get the workers up there? And the tools?"

But Borglum was a man who would not give up. He had a dream and was determined to make his dream come true.

The job would not be easy. Mount Rushmore was located miles from the nearest town with no roads leading to it, only a few logging trails through the forests.

The first thing to do was to build a road from the little town of Keystone, three miles away, to the top of the mountain. It was over this road that supplies and equipment would have to be hauled.

The people in Keystone were excited at the idea of putting up a monument in their mountains. They wanted to be part of the whole thing.

"We want to help build the road up the hill to Mount Rushmore," they said.

So everyone in the town joined in. They had a working "bee," as it was called in those days. The men struggled to cut down the trees and haul them away. Then they cleared and smoothed the roadway so cars could drive over it.

The women worked together fixing lunch for everyone. When noontime came the men stopped work for a while and ate lunch. The children helped where they could — and played a little, too, of course.

When the road was finished, workers started hauling supplies to the base of Mount Rushmore. But here they found they had another problem. The road from Keystone came only to the base of the rock where they would be working. Somehow they had to get all the tools and equipment up on top of that huge pile of rock.

So they built the first crude stairway up the side.

They did this by taking tall, straight pine trees and cutting off the branches. This left only the trunks of the trees, which were then attached by cleats into the crevices (or cracks) in the rock. The men climbed that ladder every day to go to work until later, when they built a regular stairway. Then every morning they climbed 760 steps to get to their workplace, and in the evenings they came down the same 760 steps to go

home.

On that first trip up on the pine-tree ladder the men carried with them some heavy rope and a small winch. It was a hard job to get that heavy thing up the ladder, and it took several men lifting and pulling with all their might. Finally, though, they got the winch to the top, where they fastened it to the solid rock.

Winding the rope around the winch, they then ran it back down to the bottom of the rock, where other workers tied it to some heavy steel cable. Once they pulled this cable up and attached it to the winch, they had a sturdy line from the ground to the top of the rock.

It was from this line — or cable — that a "tram," or cable car was hung and run on a pulley. This tram, which was sort of a box made of boards, had a large ore bucket on it, from the local mines. In this bucket was put the tools, dynamite, drinking water, men's lunches and other supplies to be carried up to the workplace.

When the tram was loaded, the winchman turned the handle and the cable was reeled in, pulling the tram all the way to the top.

For some time the tram was used only for supplies, but after a while it was improved to carry the workers back and forth. This saved a great deal of time and effort, since they did not then have the long climb to work each day.

Not everyone used the tram, however. A few workers decided they wanted to walk, since riding the tram was a little scary at times. It swayed back and forth in the wind, and it gave them an uneasy feeling to be hanging out in space several hundred feet above the ground!

Opposite page: The tram carrying two men nears the platform at the top of the rock. Made like a wooden box, the tram was suspended from a pulley which ran on a cable.

Chapter Three

Once the tools and supplies were on top of the rock, actual work on the carvings could begin. But what, exactly, should be carved on the mountain? The space was so big that a statue of one man would not show up well.

Since this was to be a tribute to our great country, it was finally decided to include the faces of four men — George Washington, Thomas Jefferson, Abraham Lincoln and Theodore Roosevelt.

These four men had played a big part in the building of our country. It was only right that they should be chosen to tell us of its greatness. Their faces on the mountain would remind people of America's history; it would make them proud to be Americans. This is why Mount Rushmore has come to be known as the "Shrine of Democracy."

Washington was chosen because he stands for our country's independence. Jefferson worked for a "government by the people" and was responsible for the Louisiana Purchase, which expanded our country. Lincoln saved the union for us. Roosevelt was responsible for building the Panama Canal, and he knew the value of the western part of the United States in developing our nation.

This kind of sculpture could not be done in the usual way, with a chisel and hammer, where the sculptor chipped away at a piece of stone to form a figure. This mountain was too big for that.

On an earlier project Borglum had found a way to use dynamite to blast away unneeded rock. This is the method he used at Mount Rushmore.

The first step he took was to figure out exactly where each face was going to be placed. The faces had to be where there were no cracks in the granite rock, or no flaws (bad spots). This was so that the statues would last for thousands of years without cracking or breaking off.

During construction nine different changes were made in the way the faces were placed. After Washington's face was started, for example, Borglum decided that it needed to get more light, and it was turned so that the sun fell on it for a longer time each day.

At first, Jefferson was placed on Washington's right side, and in early pictures this can still be seen. When the workers came across some poor quality rock in that spot it was decided that Jefferson would have to be put somewhere else. The partly finished Jefferson face was then blasted away and re-done on the left side of Washington.

There were several kinds of jobs to be done in carving this huge piece of rock. There were the drillers, who drilled holes in the rock for dynamite. There were dynamite men who prepared the explosive charges. There were blacksmiths who made and sharpened the drill bits used for making the holes in the rock. There were winchmen who ran the winches that lowered the workers over the edge and placed them in the spots where they needed to be. These and many others were used in the job of carving the four faces on the mountain.

Opposite: Four men in bosun's seats do some drilling during early work on Washington's nose.

Chapter Four

Men who were miners, lumberjacks, ranchers and others were hired and trained in the work on the mountain. The miners understood about blasting rock and some of them had worked with explosives before. These men were trained by Borglum to be sculptors, but the tools they used were explosives.

When first starting a carving, the men needed to blast away larger pieces of rock. In the early stages of work as much as a hundred tons at a time were blasted off. For these larger pieces a larger charge of dynamite was used. Later, when they needed to work a little more closely they used smaller dynamite charges.

Before the dynamite could be used, however, holes needed to be drilled to put the dynamite in. The holes were drilled very carefully and placed in the rock one row above another row. This drilling process was called "honeycombing" because when it was finished, the rock looked like a honeycomb in a beehive. When the drilling was done, dynamite was put in the holes to blast away just the right amount of rock. The amount of dynamite used depended upon how much rock was to be done away with.

They learned to remove exactly the right amount of stone and no more at exactly the right spot. Sometimes the workers used only blasting caps and no powder. In this way they could come as close as two or three inches from

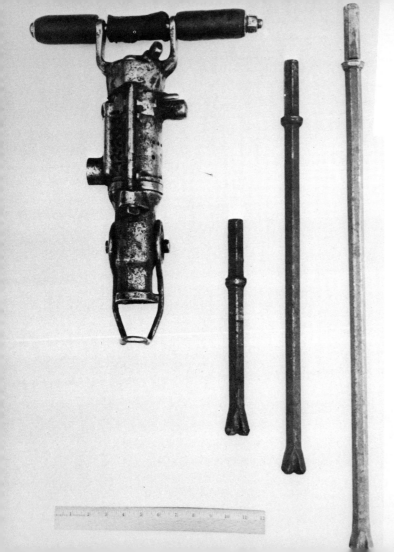

where they wanted to be.

By the time the whole job was finished they had blasted off some 500,000 tons of rock, which lay in the rubble pile below.

The blasting was done twice a day, at lunchtime and at 4 p.m., when work had stopped for the day. The workers were all away from the work area at those times and would not be in any danger. Many people found the sight of the explosion very exciting. Each time there would be crowds watching as, with a crashing roar and a billowing white cloud of dust, huge chunks of rock went tumbling and smashing onto the rubble pile below.

Opposite: The air-powered drill was used to drill holes for the dynamite. The drill bits, shown on the right, were various lengths, depending on how deep the hole was to be drilled. Notice the ruler, which gives an idea of how big the drill and bits were.

In the many years of construction there was only one blasting accident. A sudden mountain storm came up, but it seemed so far away that no one paid much attention to it. A worker was preparing the dynamite for the next blasting when a sudden bolt of lightning set it off! Fortunately, he was only slightly hurt, but after that a rule was made that all work with dynamite would stop when a lightning storm was in the area.

Opposite: Standing in the movable cage, the driller bores rows of holes to "honeycomb" the rock. Notice that the heavy drill is attached to a chain. This is so the driller did not have to hold the full weight of the drill, and so that it could not be dropped.

Opposite: A "powderman" prepares charges of dynamite to use in blasting off unwanted rock. A model of the Washington head is on the wall.

Chapter Five

Borglum had designed a special seat — called a "bosun's chair" — for the workers to use. It looked something like a seat in a swing and was made of steel and leather. It had straps to hold a man inside in case he got dizzy or became unconscious. That way he could never fall out of it.

The chair was attached at the top to a cable which ran from a winch at the top of the rock. The man who ran the winch — called a "winchman" — would turn the handle to raise or lower the chair until it was in front of the spot being worked on.

When the worker needed to change to a different spot the winchman let out more cable, or shortened it, to move the chair. Since this was before the days of walkie-talkies, there was a man known as the "callboy" who perched at the topmost edge of the carving. He was hooked to a strong harness so he wouldn't fall.

From where he sat he could see the worker and also the winchman. When the worker needed to be moved, he called up to the callboy, who then yelled up to the winchman to give him the message. Later, the callboy was given a microphone so he could talk more easily to the winchman.

Each day, when a driller got ready to start work, he climbed into the bosun's chair and strapped himself in. Making sure he had all his tools with him, he gave the signal to the winch-

In the winch house workers man the winches used to lower and raise the bosun's chairs.

man to lower him out over the edge of the rock.

As the winchman slowly turned the winch to drop him out into space, way, way above the ground, the driller looked at the people so very far below him. They looked like little ants scurrying around.

Sometimes the work he was doing needed to be done standing up rather than sitting. In that case he would go down over the side on a "movable cage," which allowed the worker to stand up and work the drill or any other tools. The cage had a railing built on three sides so that a man wouldn't step off.

Opposite: Gutzon Borglum, sculptor of Mount Rushmore, is shown in a bosun's chair. Much of the work of carving at Mount Rushmore was done by workmen who were lowered over the face of the rock in bosun's chairs. Hanging in these swing seats, workmen would drill and blast to remove unwanted rock from the mountain.

Winters in South Dakota can be very cold, but the men kept on working. On bitter cold days they covered the cage with canvas and used a small wood heater made from an oil drum, or barrel. In this way they kept warm enough to be able to work right through the winter.

The driller had an air-operated, or "pneumatic" drill which weighed 60 lbs. By standing on the movable cage or sitting in the bosun chair and bracing his feet against the rock he could drill holes into the surface. He drilled many rows of holes, one row above another, to honeycomb the rock.

The holes were drilled at different depths, some as deep as ten feet. But more often they were about two feet deep. The granite rock was so hard that a drill bit could be used for only one hole before it had to be removed from the drill and sent back to the blacksmith shop for sharpening. Over 400 drill bits were used and sharpened each day.

Sometimes the drill bits fell out and dropped hundreds of feet to the rubble pile below. For this reason, a worker was always placed so that no one was working below him. In that way, if something dropped it would not hit anyone working below.

Every few days some of the men went down to the rubble pile to collect all the drill bits that had fallen. These were returned to the blacksmith shop where they were sharpened and taken back to be used again.

After the correct number of holes were drilled they were filled with the right amount of dynamite. When several holes had been prepared and everyone was safely out of the way, a remote control lever was pressed and all the dynamite exploded at the same time.

Chapter Six

Borglum had a studio with huge windows that looked up at the carvings. From here he could see what was being done and could tell if the work was going right.

In the studio he built a model of the four figures. From these figures he could take a measurement, and what measured one foot on the model would be 12 feet on the monument above. One man — a "pointer" — took measurements from the model then traveled to the workplace above and marked out the stone with paint to show where it should be cut away. From these painted marks the workers knew where to drill.

After the larger pieces of unwanted rock had been blasted away, it was time to do the closer work. The driller, standing in the movable cage and bracing himself against the drill, bored rows of holes. Then, using a hammer and chisel, or smaller drills, workers knocked off blocks of the honeycombed granite.

As one old-timer said in describing it, "We just took a hammer and whacked it off!"

In this way the more detailed areas — like Roosevelt's mustache and the mole on Lincoln's cheek — were carefully carved. Roosevelt's mustache is 20 feet across and Lincoln's mole is 16 inches wide. The whole sculpture is 365 feet across at its widest point and 160 feet from the top of the heads to the lowest point on the coats.

The final step in the carving process was to

Roosevelt's face is set deep in the rock. It is being worked on while Lincoln's face is nearly completed.

"polish" or smooth the surface of each face. This was done by using an air-driven tool called a "bumper." This tool, which used square-ended steel bits, bounced up and down on the surface of the stone, chipping away tiny pieces until the whole area was smooth.

The men were all proud of the safety record during the years of work on the mountain, when there were only two accidents. One was the time the lightning set off the dynamite. The other was a tram accident. Five men were in the tram going to work and were close to the top. Suddenly, the cable pulley gave way and the tram went racing toward the ground! Desperately, all five men pushed on the emergency brake, but the handle broke off in their hands.

Opposite: The "callboy," safely secured by a harness, sits at the edge of one of the heads so he can call messages from the drillers to the winchman. See how far it is to the ground.

Thinking quickly, the foreman at the winch grabbed a two-by-four and jammed it between the cable and the wheel of the winch. This caused the tram to slow down enough so that the men were only shaken up a bit when it hit the ground.

Only one man was really hurt. Jumping from the car when it was still up in the air, he suffered some broken bones. When he got well, however, he went back on the job and worked until the sculpture was finished.

Opposite page: Shortly before work on the faces was finished the workplace was a busy area. Workmen can be seen in bosun's chairs and in movable cages. The buildings on top of the heads are used for equipment and for workshops. Ladders go down to several work areas.

Opposite: A worker in a bosun's chair perches on the tip of Washington's nose, while others are in the work area on top of the head.

Chapter Seven

Today the four faces on the mountain look down in silence, exactly as they did when Borglum last saw them. The broken pieces of granite blasted away from the rock still form a pile of rubble beneath the statues. A few pine trees have grown up in that pile of rock and seem to be reaching up toward Washington, Jefferson, Roosevelt and Lincoln. Other huge Ponderosa pines in the forest have grown so large that in some places they block the view from below.

Borglum had planned to add more to the figures — their hands and arms, their coats and ties. He had dreamed, also, of carving a huge hall of records out of the rock behind Lincoln's head. Here he wanted to put records of all ages and all peoples.

Also, he wanted to carve a long stairway of stone from the bottom to the top of the rock, so that tourists might climb up and explore.

His sudden death in 1941, however, brought the work to a halt and the statues, for the most part, remain unfinished. For a few months his son, Lincoln, carried on, but the main work on the monument stopped after that.

It had taken 14 years to complete the carving of Mount Rushmore. Only a total of six of those years was spent in actual work, however. The rest of the time there was no money and work stopped every once in a while when Borglum tried to get donations to carry on.

At one time school children even gave pennies so the work could continue. In later years, when those children were grown and had children of their own, they proudly told the story of how they helped build Mount Rushmore.

In 1934 the Congress of the United States voted to give money to finish the monument. This brought money in regularly and after that the work went on without stopping.

Now people very seldom go to the top of the heads, where once there was so much activity. Once a year maintenance men check the faces to make sure there is no damage to the rock. Using the same bosun's chairs the workers used, they swing back and forth in front of each face, looking for cracks in the stone. If any cracks are found they are filled with the same material Borglum used many years ago — granite dust, linseed oil and white lead. This seals the broken places so water cannot get in and freeze.

Sometimes Park Rangers go to the top to check the area. But other than that the only signs of life usually seen on the top of the heads is an occasional mountain goat.

Chapter Eight

If Gutzon Borglum could see the area around his famous monument today, he might be surprised. But then again, he might not, because he knew that such a monument as he planned would attract people. He would be happy to know that more than two million visitors come to Mount Rushmore each year.

Although there was no road to the mountain when he started, "...a trail can be built to it," he said, "to accommodate the thousands of tourists who will flock to this national shrine when it is finished."

The old dirt road from the little town of Keystone is now a well-marked, paved highway. The mountain itself is a National Memorial, patrolled by Park Rangers. The tourists stop at the National Park Service Visitors' Center to see films about the building of the monument. They attend the band concerts and other programs in the huge open-air theater just below the faces. They visit the modern gift shop, dining room and snack bar.

They take pictures of the chipmunks scampering about, and the mountain goats in the distance. They gaze at the towering mountains and the swaying pines. For this is a people's park; it belongs to you and to all Americans.

And so, one day when you visit Mount Rushmore and look up at the four faces on the mountain, remember how a group of strong men struggled to carve from the rock this great statue.

Remember how they labored to build roads and to carry supplies up the creaky ladders to the top.

Remember how they worked in snow and rain and freezing cold, and how they hung in cages and seats out in space some 500 feet from the ground.

Picture them riding up the tramway, swinging out over the tall pine trees with nothing between them and the ground far below.

Then you can take pride in knowing that these were your countrymen. They worked to carve for you and for all Americans four faces on the mountain, "...as close to heaven as we can,... where the wind and the rain alone shall wear them away."

Opposite: Mountain goats stand beneath Lincoln's lip, giving an idea of the size of the face.

Each year National Park Service personnel inspect the carving to see if any cracks have formed in the stone. A worker in a bosun's chair checks Lincoln's face for cracks. If he finds any he will seal them. Note the streaks across the face, which are different in color and texture in the rock.